LET'S PLAY
CHESS

ANTHONY HANSFORD
ILLUSTRATED BY JOHN BOLTON

Contents

The Board and the Chessmen

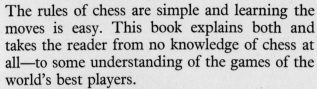

The rules of chess are simple and learning the moves is easy. This book explains both and takes the reader from no knowledge of chess at all—to some understanding of the games of the world's best players.

It teaches the reader how to read and write chess notation. This allows you to follow other people's games which is the key to understanding the game. All you need is a chess set, a board and an inquiring mind.

The game is a miniature war, fought between two sides—one coloured black and one coloured white. Each side has the same number of pieces; it is up to you, the player, to plan your campaign, decide on your tactics, to use your men to best advantage. But first you must learn what the men are and how they may be moved. Once you have learned this you have taken the first step into an exciting new world that you can explore happily all your life.

What the chessmen are worth

When you start to play chess it is useful to have a rough guide to the value of the pieces but remember that it is only a rough guide.

Queen = 9 pawns.
Rook   = 5 pawns.
Bishop = 3 pawns.
Knight = 3 pawns.

We do not give a value for the King. **If you lose the King then you have lost the game.**

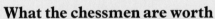

Look at **Fig A.** White is playing up the board in the direction of the arrow. His right-hand corner square is White.

Black is playing in the opposite direction, down the board. His right-hand corner square is also white. This is the first rule of chess. You must have a white square at the right-hand corner of the board. Look at **Fig B.** The arrows are going across the board. Each arrow lies along a row of eight squares. These rows are called 'ranks'. Look at **Fig C.** This time the arrows are going up and down the board. Each arrow lies along a line of eight squares. The lines are called 'files'.

So the chessboard has eight ranks each made up of eight squares and eight files each made up of eight squares, so as each rank or file has eight squares and as there are eight ranks or files and as 8 x 8 = 64, then the chessboard must have 64 squares.

As you move along a rank or up and down a file, each square you come to is a different colour to the one next to it. Half are White and the other half Black. So 32 squares on the board are White (or light coloured) and 32 squares are Black (or dark coloured).

Look at **Fig D.** The arrows are slanting across the board. Each square under the arrow is the same colour. These slanting lines of squares are called diagonals.

The type of chess set in the picture is called a Staunton pattern chess set. It was named after a famous English player of the early 19th century. There are hundreds of different types of chess sets but this one, the Staunton pattern, is the only one used for serious games. Look at **Fig E.** It is exactly the same as the picture of the real chess set. We call this sort of chess picture, a diagram. In chess diagrams, White is always at the bottom, playing up the board and Black is at the top, playing down the board.

Throughout this book the White pieces are represented in red and the Black in blue.

The board is always set out in exactly the same way at the start of a game as shown on **Figs F – J.**

Fig F. These are the Rooks which always start off in the corner squares.

Fig G. Now we add the Knights which always start off standing next to the Rooks.

Fig H. Now we add the Bishops which stand next to the Knights.

Fig I. Now we add the Queens which always stand on a square of their own colour. Therefore, the White Queen stands on a White square and the Black Queen on a Black square.

Fig J. Now we add the Kings which stand next to the Queens.

Lastly we add eight pawns for each side. That takes us back to **Fig E** and now all the chessmen are set out on the board ready to begin the game.

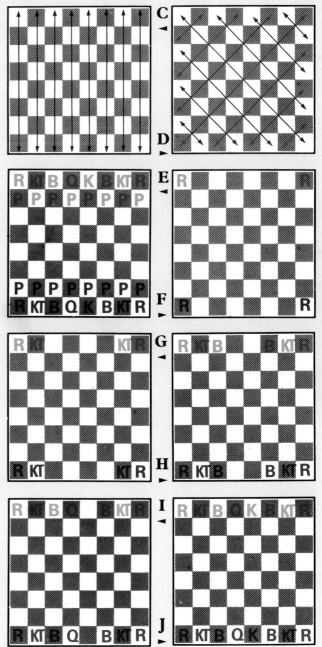

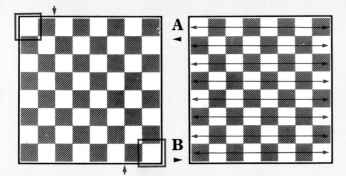

How the Chessmen Move-1

The King

The King is the tallest and the most important man on the board. His move is simple—one square at a time in any direction. If we put the King in the middle of the board (**Fig A**) he can move to eight different squares. On a corner he can move to three squares (**Fig B**).

In **Fig C** the King can only move to four squares as he cannot move to the square on his left which is already occupied by his own Queen. Two men cannot stand on the same square at the same time.

In **Fig D** the King can move to five squares. He can move to the same four squares as before, and because this time the Queen on his left belongs to his opponent, he can capture by placing his King on the square occupied by the Queen and taking the Queen off the board.

The Queen

The Queen stands next to the King at the start of the game on a square of her own colour. She is almost as tall as the King, but not quite so important because the game can carry on even if the Queens are off the board.

The Queen is the strongest piece on the board. She can move to as many squares as she wants in any direction.

If we put the Queen in the middle of the board (**Fig E**) look at how many squares she can reach—27.

Even on a corner square (**Fig F**) she can move to 21 squares which is much further than the King.

The Queen captures just like the King. If one of the enemy men stands on a square that she can reach in one move, she moves to that

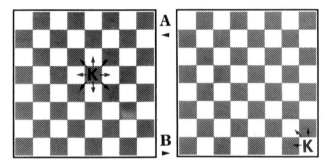

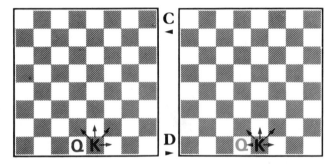

square and takes the enemy man off the board. (**Fig G**).

In **Fig H** you can see that the Queen can get hemmed in by her own men.

The Bishop

There are two Bishops on each side which start off the game on either side of the King and Queen. This means that one Bishop starts on a Black square and the other on a White square.

This is very important because the Bishop always moves on the same colour square as he starts on.

From the middle of the board (**Fig I**), the Bishop can move to 13 squares all of which are the same colour. The Bishop moves slantwise up and down the board in a line known as a diagonal.

In **Fig J**, the Bishop on a corner square can only move on one diagonal—to seven squares.

When you are playing chess you must be careful not to hem in your men. Remember, pieces apart from knights cannot jump over other men.

Bishops, like other pieces, capture by moving to the square occupied by the opposing piece and take it off the board. You do not **have** to capture in chess unless you want to, except in special cases which we will explain later.

You may wonder why there is a piece called a Bishop in a war game like Chess. Long ago, as well as being religious leaders, Bishops often led armies into battle.

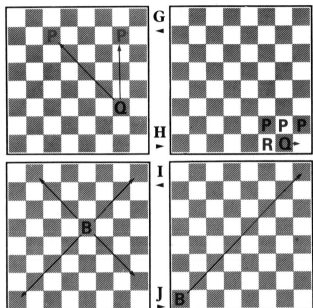

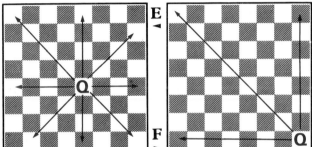

How the Chessmen Move-2

The Rook

Each player has two Rooks which start the game from the corner squares. The Rook on the Queen's side is called the Queen's Rook and the one on the King's side is the King's Rook.

The Rook moves as many squares as it likes on ranks and files but never on diagonals. In **Fig A**, the Rook can move to 14 squares, and even on the corner square the Rook can still move to 14 squares if nothing else gets in the way (**Fig B**).

Now look at **Fig C**. The Rook can only move onto two squares.

The Rook captures just like the other pieces; simply by moving him onto the square previously occupied by the piece you are taking and

removing the captured piece (**Fig D**).

Rooks work best in a game when they defend each other. As you will see in games that follow, they can attack together down a file (**Fig E**), or along a rank (**Fig F**).

The Knight

Each player has two Knights which stand between the Rook and Bishop at the start.

Most beginners find the Knight's move the hardest to learn but it's really very easy. Look

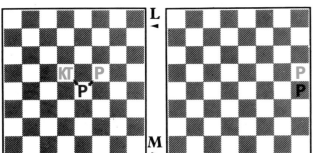

at **Fig G**. The Knight can move to any of the squares marked. Two squares up and one to the side making an L-shape. Look at **Fig H**. Because of its move, two up and one to the side, the Knight can jump over the pawns. It is the only piece which can do this. In the starting position it is the only piece which can move before a pawn moves.

As we have seen, the Knight can reach eight squares from a centre square. Look at **Fig I**. Now it can only move to four squares. Compare this with **Fig G**, where it can move to eight squares. You will see in the games that follow that you must place your Knights where they can do the most good. That is nearly always near the centre and not at the edge of the board. The Knight captures just like the other pieces. Look at **Fig J**. When the Knight takes the Bishop, you simply remove the Bishop from the board and place the Knight on the square the Bishop was occupying. The move to take the Bishop was two squares up and one to the side, just the same as its normal move.

The Pawn

Each player has eight pawns. One stands in front of each of the other pieces at the beginning of the game (see page 13 **Fig C**) and is named after that piece. All the pawns move the same way. One square forward at a time, except for the first move when they can be moved two squares forward if one wishes. **Fig K** shows the first move in a game. White has played his King's pawn two squares forward down the King's file and Black has played his Queen's pawn one square forward down the Queen's file.

The pawns can only go forward.

Again, unlike all the other chessmen, pawns capture in a different way from their normal move. Look at **Fig L**. The White pawn can capture either the Black pawn or the Knight. It simply moves one square forward diagonally, to the square of the pawn or the Knight.

As pawns capture by moving one square diagonally forward, this means that two opposing pawns on the same file will block each other (**Fig M**).

Because pawns cannot retreat and can block each other, the way they are moved is very important. As you can see in **Fig N**, none of the pieces can move very far and some can not move at all. Look at **Fig O**. Here some of the pawns have been captured and now all the pieces can move easily. In both cases, it is the way that the pawns have been moved which has decided what sort of game will result.

Check and Checkmate

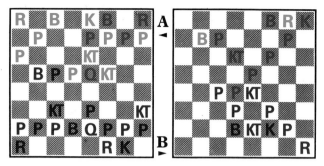

If you make a move which threatens to take your opponent's King, then his King is in **check** (**Fig A**).

If he did nothing about it, you would simply take his King with your Bishop and win the game because capturing your opponent's King wins the game. The rules of chess say that when your King is in check, you must make a move at once which gets it out of check. Look at **Fig A** again. There are three different moves which Black can make to get out of check. Firstly he can put his own Bishop between his King and the White Bishop. This blocks the check. In chess this is called 'interposing'. Secondly,

he can capture the White Bishop with his pawn. Once the Bishop is off the board his King is no longer in any danger. Thirdly, he can move his King to a safe square. In this diagram that would be to the square where his Queen stands at the start of the game. Which move would you make? Taking the Bishop would be best. You would get one of the White pieces for nothing and White would have one less to play with.

Look at **Fig B**. Black is in check again. What move can he make to get out of check? There is not one. He cannot take the White Rook. He has no piece to block the check (interpose). He cannot move his King to a square where he would not still be in check. He has lost. Whatever move Black made, White would then play his Rook and take the King. In fact the game stops one move before that. If a King is in check and there is no move to get him out of the check, then that is called checkmate. Checkmate is the end of the game. If you checkmate your opponent, you have won.

So now we know that the purpose of the game

is to checkmate one's opponent, and we know how the pieces move. Let's play a game.

Look at **Fig C**. The right hand corner square is White. The White Queen is standing on a White square. The Black Queen on a Black square. All is correct. Sometimes you can get the starting position for the Knights and Bishops mixed up. They are all right in **Fig C**.

Fig D. White always moves first in chess. Remember that he could move the pawn one **or** two squares forward on his first move.

Now Black makes his first move (**Fig E**).

Fig F. White moves second pawn.

Fig G. Black Queen moves . . . Checkmate! There's nothing White can do. This game is the shortest one possible in chess. It's called 'Fool's Mate'.

Let's look at a second game, 'Scholar's Mate'. **Fig H, Fig I, Fig J, Fig K, Fig L, Fig M, Fig N**. These games teach two very important lessons. Firstly, the square in front of your King's Bishop is your weakest point. Always be on your guard if your opponent moves a piece to attack that square as White did in **Fig K**. Secondly, the diagonal marked with a red arrow in **Fig G** is also a weak point.

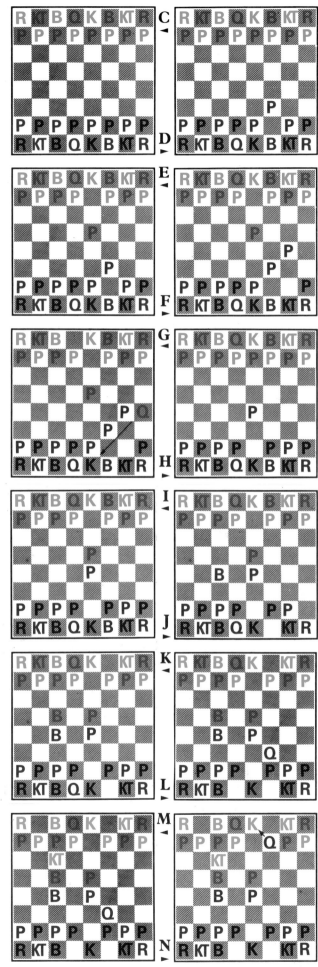

Understanding Chess Diagrams

If you wanted to remember a game so that you could show someone else, how would you do it?

You could not draw a picture of the board with all the pieces for each move like the diagrams in this book. It would take too long.

If it was a short game you might be able to remember it all by looking very carefully, but you would not be able to do that for a longer game.

This was the problem that faced chess players many years ago. Their solution was to use a code or form of short-hand.

To record a chess move you have to know two things. First, which of the chessmen is being moved and second, where it is going. Let's record the 'Fool's Mate' we were looking at in the section on 'Check and Checkmate'. Compare the diagrams with these moves.

White's first move: Pawn in front of the Bishop next to the King—forward one square.

Black's first move: Pawn in front of the King —forward two squares. White's second move: Pawn in front of the Knight nearest to the King —forward two squares.

Black's second move: Queen to the fifth square in front of the Rook nearest to the King. Checkmate!

This is clear enough but it's too long-winded. **Fig A** shows how we indicate where a piece or pawn is going. Each square has it's own CODE letters and number.

On the first rank the squares are numbered

A

8 QR8	QKT8	QB8	Q8	K8	KB8	KKT8	KR8
7 QR7	QKT7	QB7	Q7	K7	KB7	KKT7	KR7
6 QR6	QKT6	QB6	Q6	K6	KB6	KKT6	KR6
5 QR5	QKT5	QB5	Q5	K5	KB5	KKT5	KR5
4 QR4	QKT4	QB4	Q4	K4	KB4	KKT4	KR4
3 QR3	QKT3	QB3	Q3	K3	KB3	KKT3	KR3
2 QR2	QKT2	QB2	Q2	K2	KB2	KKT2	KR2
1 QR1	QKT1	QB1	Q1	K1	KB1	KKT1	KR1

one. The second rank are numbered two and so on.

The first 'file' is named after the Queen's Rook or QR because in the starting position that's where it stands. The second file after the Queen's Knight or QKT, and so on through the Queen or Q and King or K to the eighth file named after the King's Rook or KR. The pieces too are identified in the same way by their initials, e.g. K = King, QB = Queen's Bishop.

The Pawns are all identified by the initials of the piece in front of which they stand at the starting position. For example, Queen's Rook Pawns = QRP and the King's Pawn = KP.

Let's record the second game from the chapter on 'Check and Checkmate' using this system called 'Descriptive Notation'. Compare the moves with the diagrams on page 13 for 'Scholar's Mate'.

WHITE	BLACK
1. P–K4	P–K4
2. B–B4	B–B4
3. Q–B3	KT–QB3
4. Q x P mate.	

You can see that a dash (–) means that a piece or pawn moves to a square and that a cross (x) means a piece or pawn captured. **Fig B** is a chessboard prepared for another system called 'Algebraic Notation'. In this system 'Fool's Mate' would be recorded as follows:

WHITE	BLACK
1. f2–f3	e7–e5
2. g2–g4	Qd8–h4 mate.

Only the pieces are indicated by their initial letter as you can see. When a pawn moves only the squares involved are shown.

Descriptive Notation is the system chiefly in use in the English speaking countries.

B ►

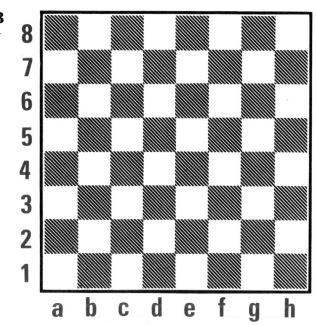

Special Moves-1

The first special move we are going to look at is called 'castling'. You can castle on the King's side (which is shown in our chess code as O–O) or on the Queen's side (which is shown as O–O–O).

In castling you move two of your own pieces at the same time. These are the King and the Rook. Look at **Fig A.** The White King and King's Rook are preparing to castle on the King's side. The King moves two squares to the right. At the same time the King's Rook moves two squares to the left. After castling on the King's side, the King will be standing on KKT1, and the Rook on KB1. Black has castled on the King's side already in **Fig A.** Now for castling on the Queen's side (**Fig B**).

Once again the King moves two squares but this time to the left (the Queen's side). The Queen's Rook at the same time moves three squares to the right. After castling on the Queen's side, the King will be standing on QB1 and the Queen's Rook on Q1. Black has castled on the Queen's side already in **Fig B.**

You have already seen some of the main rules of chess in the section on 'Check and Checkmate'. Here are six more rules which only concern castling. You cannot castle if:—

1. You are in check.
2. You would pass through check.
3. You would end up in check.
4. You have moved your King already.
5. You have already moved the Rook with which you had planned to castle.
6. Any of the squares between the King and Rook are occupied.

Look at **Fig C.** In this position White cannot castle because the Black Rook controls White's KB1 square. The White King would have to pass through this square in castling, which is not allowed. He would be passing through check (RULE 2).

If the Black Rook in **Fig C** was standing on KKT8, then White still would not be able to castle. If he did the King would finish up in check. You can't castle into check (RULE 3).

Castling is a very important move in chess and is often played early in the game. It gets the King to safety and brings the Rook into the game.

Here is a short game where White discovers checkmate as he castles. In this game the American, Paul Morphy, was giving his opponent the advantage by playing without his Queen's Rook.

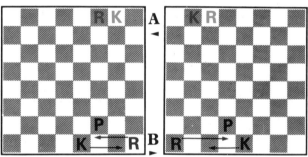

WHITE	BLACK
P. Morphy	Amateur

TWO KNIGHT'S DEFENCE

1. P–K4	P–K4
2. KT–KB3	KT–QB3

When writing White's second move, you have to show which of his two Knights was moved. By showing that it was moved to KB3, it is clear that it was the King's Knight. With Black's second move the QB3 square shows that the Queen's Knight was moved.

3. B–B4	KT–B3

On White's third move, only one Bishop can be played, to B4, so **3. B–B4** is all you have to write. With Black's third move only one Knight can still be played to B3, so **3 . . . . . . , KT–B3** is sufficient.

4. KT–KT5	. . . . . .

The Knight moves again. You can see that White is threatening to take Black's Bishop's Pawn and call check (**B x P ch**), or take Black's

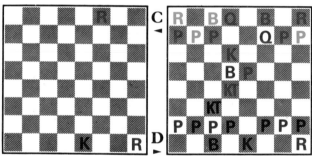

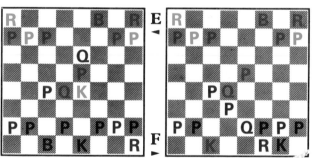

Bishop's Pawn with his Knight (**KT x BP**)? The dotted line where Black's move should be shows that this note is only concerned with White's fourth move. Black's fourth move is next.

4.	**P–Q4**	(Here it is)
5. **P x P**	**KT x P**	
6. **KT x BP**	......	

Because the White Knight could take two different pawns (the Bishop's or the Rook's) you have to show which one he did take, in this case the King's Bishop pawn.

| 6. ...... | **K x KT** |
| 7. **Q–B3 ch** | ...... |

The White Queen checks the King and at the same time threatens to take the Black Knight on the next move.

| 7. ...... | **K–K3** |

The Black King defends his Knight.

8. **KT–B3**	**KT–Q5**
9. **B x KT ch**	**K–Q3**
10. **Q–B7 (Fig D)**	......

Does your own board have the same position as **Fig D**? If it does then you have followed the descriptive notation correctly, remembering that White was playing without the Queen's Rook. White now threatens to mate black with his next move.

10.	**B–K3**
11. **B x B**	**KT x B**
12. **KT–K4 ch**	**K–Q4**
13. **P–B4 ch**	**K x KT**
14. **Q x KT**	**Q–Q5 (Fig E)**

Does your board have the same position as **Fig E**? You have to be very careful when making Black's moves as you must count the squares from the other side of the board.

15. **Q–KT4 ch**	**K–Q6**
16. **Q–K2 ch**	**K–B7**
17. **P–Q3 ch**	**K x B**
18. **O–O mate (Fig F)**	

White castled King's side (**O–O**) and checkmated Black at the same time, most unusual.

17

Special Moves-2

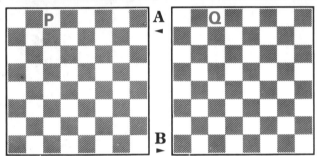

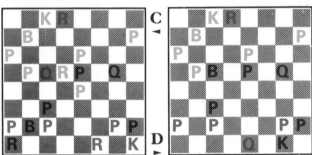

When a pawn gets to the eighth rank (**Fig A**) it is promoted to any piece except the King. Usually it is promoted to a Queen.

In **Fig B**, White has chosen to promote his pawn to a Queen. This is often called 'Queen-ing'. In our descriptive notation chess code the move in **Fig A** and **B** would be **P–B8=Q.**

This ability to change into a Queen can make a pawn very important, especially towards the end of the game when most of the pieces have been taken off the board. The nearer the pawn gets to the eighth rank, the more important it becomes. Look at **Fig C**. It is Black to move.

1. . . . . . .   **P–K6**

The Black pawn pushes forward. Only two squares to go before it Queens. What makes it even more dangerous is that it is a 'passed pawn', one which can never be blocked or taken by an enemy pawn. As you can see in **Fig C**, White does not have a pawn which can take or block Black's King's pawn.

2. QR–K1   . . . . . .

We have to say which Rook moves to K1. Now you can see why the passed pawn is so dangerous. White has to use a Rook to block it. That means a whole Rook is being used to block a pawn. This is waste of a piece but White has to try to stop the pawn with something.

2. . . . . . .   **R–Q7**

You will see this move with the Rook in lots of games. It is called a 'seventh rank invasion'. Once a Rook gets to the seventh rank it will find plenty of targets. Here Black threatens to take the Knight's Pawn with his Rook, for example. Did you notice that Black's Rooks were operating together down the Queen's file?

3. R–KKT1   **P–K7**

4. B–B1   . . . . . .

White threatens to take the Black Rook.

4. . . . . . .   **R–Q8**

White cannot play **5. R x P** because of **5.** . . . . . . , **Q x R mate.** He cannot play **5. R x R** because then **5.** . . . . , **R x R, 6. R x R, P x R =Q mate.**

5. B–K3   . . . . . .

White threatens the Queen.

5. . . . . . .   **R x R**

6. B x Q   **R x R ch**

7. K x R   **P–K8=Q mate.** (Fig D)

So the passed pawn 'Queens' and delivers mate. White's seventh move was a blunder. We show bad mistakes like that in chess notation with a question mark. He should have played **7. B x R.** He would still have lost though.

Here's a famous opening trap where a pawn

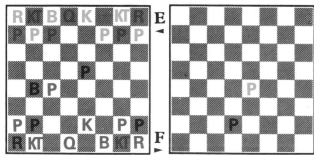

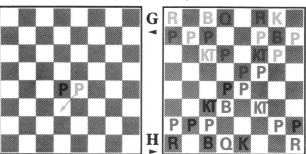

is promoted. The opening is called 'The Albin Counter Gambit'.

1. P–Q4, P–Q4; 2. P–QB4, P–K4; 3. P x KP, P–Q5; 4. P–K3, B–KT5 ch; 5. B–Q2, P x P; 6. B x B, P x P ch. 7. K–K2, P x KT = KT ch; (**Fig E**).

White cannot play **7. K x P** because of **7. . . . . . , Q x Q.** So Black promoted his pawn to a Knight **7. . . . . . . , P x KT=ch.** If he had queened his pawn with **7. . . . . . . , P x KT=Q** he would not have had the White King in check and White could play 8. Q x Q ch. Now as the Black pawn has become a Knight, White has to play **8. K–K1,** or lose the Queen. (If **8. R x KT, B–KT5 ch** wins the Queen.)

En Passant

Many years ago the rules of chess were altered slightly to speed up the game. One of the changes introduced was 'Castling'. Another was the choice of moving a pawn two squares forward on its first move instead of one.

It was obvious that this choice of two squares forward instead of one could be used to avoid capture by a pawn on his opponent's fifth rank, P–Q4 and his pawn would be safe (**Fig F**). To stop this, the new rule stated that if a player chose the two square forward move and thus

avoided capture by a pawn on his opponent's fifth rank, his pawn could still be captured as if it had only moved one square forward. As in **Fig G**.

Of course, one need not use the right to take 'en passant' (in passing) but if one does it must be used as the next move.

Here is a short game between two of today's grandmasters where 'en passant' is played.

WHITE	BLACK
V. Hort	J. Donner
1. P–K4	P–Q3
2. P–Q4	KT–KB3
3. KT–QB3	P–KKT3
4. P–B4	B–KT2
5. KT–B3	O–O
6. B–Q3	KT–B3
7. P–B5	P–K4 (Fig H)
8. P x P e.p.	P x P
9. O–O	Q–K2
10. Q–K1	KT–Q1
11. Q–R4	P–K4
12. KT–KKT5	P–KR3
13. B–B4 ch	K–R1
14. KT–B3	P x P
15. B x P	B–K3
16. KT–Q5	Resigns.

Drawn Games

Look at **Fig A**. It's White's move. Where can he go? He cannot move at all! Any move White makes would put his King into check and that is against the rules. But White has to move, that is also one of the rules; you're not allowed to give up your turn. So what happens now?

This is called Stalemate; the game is drawn.

Draws by Agreement

Look at **Fig B**. Neither player has enough material left to win. So a draw would be agreed. There are lots of positions in the end game where neither player can win and a draw is agreed.

Repetition of Position

Look at **Fig C**.

White plays	and Black replies
1. R–B7	**1. ......, KT–R3** (**Fig D**)

White plays	and Black replies
2. R–Q7	**2. ......, KT–B4**

So now we have the same position as **Fig C** again.

3. R–B7, KT–R3. (**Fig D** again)
4. R–Q7, ...

Here Black indicates that he will play **4. ...... KT–B4** again. This would repeat the position (**Fig C**) for the third time. He claims a draw. If Black had played this move without claiming a draw—then White could claim a draw.

The rule states that you can claim a draw after the same position has appeared three times and each time it has been the same player's move.

The 50-move rule

If at any time in the game you can prove that at least 50 moves each have been played without any pawn moves or any piece captures—then you can claim a draw. This is very rare.

Perpetual Check

Here is a game which shows the last type of drawn game. It was played in 1914 between the World Champion, Emanuel Lasker, and Alexander Alekhine who became World Champion in 1927.

WHITE	BLACK
A. Alekhine	**Em Lasker**

SCOTCH GAME

1. P–K4	P–K4

The first move for both players allows the Bishop and Queen to move.

2. KT–KB3	KT–QB3

Now White attacks the Black King's pawn with his Knight and Black defends.

| 3. P–Q4 | P x P |
| 4. KT x P | KT–B3 |

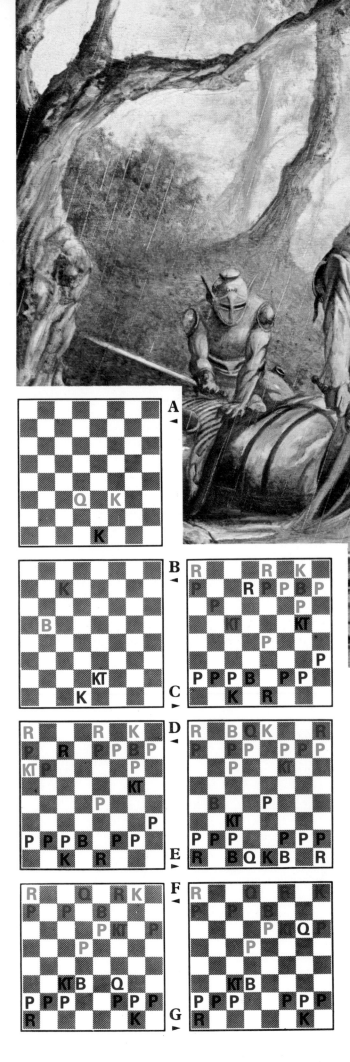

Now Black attacks White's pawn and White is forced to defend.

5. KT–QB3 . . . . . .

We have to show which Knight is being moved. The King's Knight at Q4 could move to B3.

5. . . . . . .   **B–KT5**

6. KT x KT   **KTP x KT** (Fig E)

We have to say which pawn takes the White Knight because Black could also take with the Queen's pawn. He did not want to play **6.** . . . . . . , **QP x KT**; because then White would reply **7. Q x Q, K x Q** (forced); and Black would be unable to castle.

7. B–Q3   **P–Q4**

8. P x P   **P x P**

9. O–O   **O–O**

10. B–KKT5   **B–K3**

Both players have castled and got their pieces out.

11. Q–B3   **B–K2**

12. KR–K1   **P–KR3**

With White's twelfth move, you have to show which Rook moved to K1, with Black's twelfth move, **P–R3** would not be sufficient as either pawn could move to **R3**.

13. B x P   . . . . . .

White gives up his Bishop for a pawn!

13. . . . . . .   **P x B**

14. R x B   . . . . . .

Now he gives up his Rook for a Bishop.

14. . . . . . .   **P x R** (Fig F)

So White has given up a whole Rook for a pawn.

15. Q–KT3 ch   **K–R1**

Black could not play **15.** . . . . . . , **K–B2** because

16. Q–KT6 is mate.

16. Q–KT6 (Fig G)

The game is drawn. Black cannot stop White playing **17. Q x P ch** and **18. Q–KT5 ch.** Perpetual check.

In this case White, Alekhine, played for a draw deliberately. He did not try to win.

The Traps-1

Forks

When a piece attacks two or more different targets at the same time we call that type of attack a fork.

Look at **Fig A**. The Knight attacks three different pieces at once.

In **Fig B**, the pawn attacks Bishop and Knight at the same time.

In **Fig C**, the Bishop attacks the Rook and King at the same time.

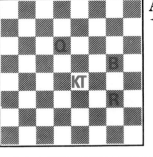

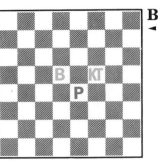

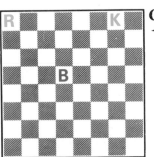

Now we are going to look at a game where the fork is used to help win the game. The game was one of a simultaneous display given by Bronstein who played Black. A simultaneous display is where one player plays against a number of other players, all at the same time

WHITE	BLACK
A. N. Other	D. Bronstein

THE KING'S GAMBIT

1. P–K4	P–K4
2. P–KB4	. . . . . .

A gambit is the offer of a piece or pawn for an advantage later on in the game. Here White offers the King's Bishop's pawn. The opening gets its name from this offer.

2.	P x P

When the pawn is taken by Black, the opening is called 'The King's Gambit Accepted'.

Now White can play **3. P–Q4**. Look at **Fig D**. He gets a very good position. Look at all the centre squares he commands. What can Black do ? He would play **3. . . . . . . , Q–R5** ch, a move we have looked at in 'Fool's Mate'.

This time it is not checkmate but look what would happen. **3. P–Q4, Q–R5 check. 4. P–KT3, P x P,** (**Fig E**). **5. P x P, Q x R.** Black would win.

So first White has to stop Black playing **3. . . . . . . Q–R5 ch.**

3. KT–KB3	. . . . . .

That stops the Black Queen.

3.	KT–KB3

Black attacks the White King's pawn.

4. P–K5	KT–R4

Now the pawn attacks the Knight.

It looks as if the Black Knight is in trouble. (**Fig F**.) What would happen if White played **5. P–KKT4** ? The Knight is trapped. It can only move to squares where a White pawn can take it. Black would take the pawn 'en passant'.

5. KT–B3	P–Q3
6. B–B4	P x P
7. KT x P	. . . . . .

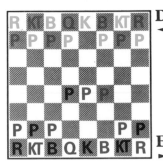

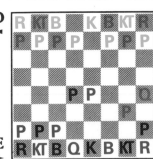

The correct move for White here is **B x P check**. The move played is a double attack. It threatens **8. KT x P** a fork on the Black Queen and Rook. It also threatens **8. Q x KT.**

7.	Q–R5 ch
8. K–B1	B–K3
9. B x B	. . . . . .

White accepts the sacrifice.

9.	KT–KT6 ch

This is the first fork. The White King and Rook are attacked at the same time (**Fig G**).

What would happen if White played **10. P x KT** ? Then Black would play **10. . . . . . . , Q x R ch;** the White Rook's pawn is pinned.

10. K–KT1	B–B4 ch

11. P–Q4   **B x P ch**
Black sacrifices another piece.

12. Q x B   **KT–K7 ch**
The second fork; the Black Knight checks the King and attacks the Queen at the same time. It's lucky for White that he can play

13. KT x KT. Or is it?

13. KT x KT   **Q–K8 mate.**
So White's reply was not good enough.

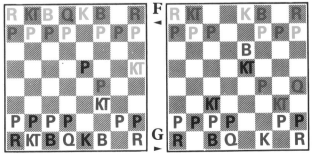

23

The Traps-2

Pins

A piece is pinned when it cannot move or when moving it would be a mistake. Look at the diagrams. In **Fig A**, if the Black Knight was to move, Black would be in check. That is not allowed so the Black Knight cannot move.

In **Fig B** the Black Rook can move. It can take the White Knight. If it did, what would White do? White would take the Black Queen, so moving the Black Rook would be a mistake.

In fact a pinned piece is useless. It cannot really move at all.

We are going to look at a very famous game where pins are used to help win the game.

WHITE	BLACK
P. Morphy	Duke of Brunswick and Count Isouard

PHILIDOR'S DEFENCE

1. P–K4   P–K4
2. KT–KB3   P–Q3

Both players can move either the Queen or King's Bishop after their first move.

White's second move threatens the Black King's pawn and Black's second move defends it. In playing 2. ......, **P–Q3** Black blocks his King's Bishop.

3. P–Q4   B–KT5 (Fig C)

The first pin. Now the White King's Knight cannot move or he loses the Queen.

4. P x P   ......

White threatens to win a pawn. If Black plays 4. ......, **P x P** then 5. Q x Q ch, K x Q; 6. KT x P.

4. ......   B x KT
5. Q x B   P x P
6. B–QB4   ......

Now White threatens checkmate on KB7. Just like the Scholar's Mate.

6. ......   KT–B3
7. Q–QKT3   ......

White threatens two things at once. He threatens 8. B x P ch. and 8. Q x P.

7. ......   Q–K2

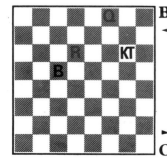
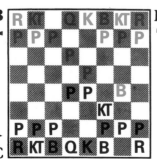
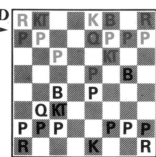

24

Black stops **8. B x P ch.** If White plays **8. Q x P** then Black can play **8. . . . . . . , Q–KT5 ch, 9. Q x Q** (this is a forced move or he loses his Queen), **B x Q** and Black is not too badly off.

8. KT–B3   **P–B3**

This move lets Black's Queen protect the Knight's pawn. It also stops a White piece landing on White's Queen 5 square.

9. B–KKT5   . . . . .

The second pin of the game. Now Black's King's Knight can't move (**Fig D**).

9. . . . . . .   **P–KT4**

Black forces the White Bishop away.

10. KT x P   . . . . .

Well! Who would have thought of that move! It looks like a mistake!

10. . . . . . .   **P x KT**

11. B x KTP ch   **QKT–Q2 (Fig E)**

Black moves his Queen's Knight between the White Bishop and his own King to stop the check. So his Queen's Knight is unable to move, and that's the third pin of the game.

Black's position is terrible. Both Knights are pinned, his Bishop can't move and his King's Rook is blocked in.

Morphy's tenth move was correct! A move like that is called a sacrifice.

12. O–O–O.   . . . . .

White brings his King to safety and attacks the Black Knight with his Rook.

12. . . . . . .   **R–Q1**

Black has to protect his Queen's Knight.

13. R x KT!   . . . . .

Another sacrifice.

13. . . . . . .   **R x R (Fig F)**

Now the Rook is pinned. The fourth pin.

14. R–Q1   . . . . .

This is almost the same position as **Fig E** except that a Black Rook is pinned.

14. . . . . . .   **Q–K3**

Black unpins his King's Knight at last and tries to exchange Queens but it's too late.

15. B x R ch   **KT x B**

Morphy finishes with a brilliant move. (**Fig G**).

16. Q–KT8 ch   **KT x Q**

17. R–Q8 ch mate.

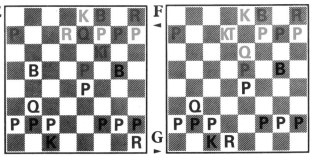

The Traps-3

Skewers

A skewer is an attack on a piece which is screened or hidden by a more important piece.

Look at **Fig A.** The Black King is in check and has to move. When the King (the screen) does move, then White takes the Rook.

Look at **Fig B.** Here the Rook is attacked. When it moves White takes the Knight.

Now we are going to look at a game which will show us how a skewer can be used. The player with the Black pieces, Alexander Alekhine, later became World Champion from 1927 to 1935 and again from 1937 until his death in 1946.

WHITE	BLACK
J. de Rodzynski	A. Alekhine

KING'S KNIGHT'S OPENING

1. P–K4   P–K4

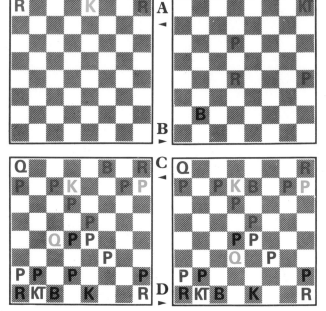

three pieces, the White Queen, Bishop and Knight attacking the Black King's Bishop's pawn.

6. ......   KT–R3

Now the King's Bishop's pawn has three defenders. Usually we would not play the Knight to the edge of the board, but this time the Knight is needed to help in the defence.

7. B x P ch   .....

White takes the pawn anyway. Let's see if his sacrifice is correct.

7. ......   KT x B

8. KT x KT   Q x KT

9. Q x P   ......

A fork! Now White attacks the Rook and the Knight at the same time. He must win one of them so it looks as if he was right to sacrifice.

9. ......   K–Q2

10. Q x R   ......

Now Black's King's Bishop is pinned; if it moves White wins the Rook.

10. ......   Q–QB5

Black threatens checkmate on White's K2 square.

11. P–B3   B x P

This seems to be a surprise sacrifice, let's see if it was correct.

12. P x B   KT–Q5!

Now Black threatens checkmate on White's K2 square again. White could take the Knight (**13. P x KT**) but what would happen if he did?

Look at **Fig C**. Black would play **13. ......, Q x B ch**. A skewer! White has to move his King and then loses his Rook.

13. P–Q3   ......

The threat of the skewer is enough. White will not take the Knight.

13. ......   Q x P

14. P x KT   .....

Black does not threaten the skewer now as he took White's Queen's pawn on his last move, so White can now take the Knight.

14. ......   B–K2

The winning move! The Black Bishop was pinned and if it moved the Black lost the Rook. But why did Alekhine move it? Look at **Fig D**.

15. Q x R   B–R5 mate

The pin on the Bishop was a false pin. Black's move **14. ......, B–K2** was a discovered attack on the Queen. Because of the threat **15. ......, B–R5** mate, White's Queen was lost.

So Black, two Rooks and one Knight behind in material, wins by checkmate. An important lesson to remember. Material isn't always everything.

2. KT–KB3   KT–QB3

3. B–B4   P–Q3

Black's reply is not often played to-day. Normally Black would play **3. ......, KT–B3**, an opening called 'The Two Knight's Defence'.

4. P–B3   ......

This is a bit slow. Better would be **4. P–Q4**.

4. ......   B–KT5

This move pins the White Knight.

5. Q–KT3   ......

This is the same move that Paul Morphy used against the Duke and Count. It attacks the Queen's Knight's pawn and the King's Bishop's pawn at the same time. A double attack.

5. ......   Q–Q2

Alekhine defends his King's Bishop's pawn.

6. KT–KT5   ......

White piles on the pressure. There are now

Discovered and Double Check

Discovered check is one of the most dangerous moves you can make in a game. Look at **Fig A**. If White plays **1. KT–Q6** then Black is in check. A discovered check. After Black moves, White then plays **2. KT x R**.

The discovered check is really the opposite of a 'Pin'. Look at **Fig A** again. If the Knight in the diagram was a Black Knight it would be pinned. It would not be able to move at all, would it? Now because the Knight is White, it can move anywhere. Even to a square like Q6 where normally it would be taken by the pawn on K7. Black does not have time to take it because of the check by the Bishop.

Double check is really a discovered check where the piece moved (discovering the check) also makes a check.

Now look at **Fig B**. White plays **1. R–B8**. A double check. Check with the Rook and Bishop

at the same time. In fact it is checkmate. There's nothing Black can do. He cannot play **1. . . . . . . , R x R** because he would still be in check from the Bishop. He can't block the check with **1. . . . . . . , B–K1** because if he blocks the check by the Rook, then the check by the Bishop remains. He cannot block the Bishop check with **1. . . . . . . , B–B2** because the Rook check would still be there. When a double check is played the King always has to move. You can not take or block two checks at once. If the King cannot move then it must be checkmate. Double check is the most deadly trap of all.

Here is a short game showing both traps. It was played in a five minute game between the American master Edward Lasker (not to be confused with Emanuel Lasker the World Champion from 1894 to 1921) and Sir George Thomas in 1912.

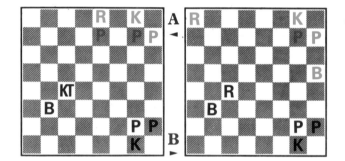

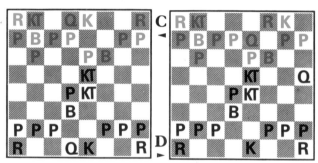

WHITE	BLACK
Ed Lasker	Sir George
	Thomas

DUTCH DEFENCE

1. P–Q4	P–KB4
2. KT–KB3	P–K3
3. KT–QB3	KT–KB3

Black always has to defend against the threat of **Q–R5** in this opening. This is because he has moved his King's Bishop pawn. (Remember that from 'Fool's Mate').

4. B–KT5	B–K2
5. B x KT	B x B
6. P–K4	P x P
7. KT x P	. . . . . .

Now Black's defending Knight at KB3 has gone.

7.	P–QKT3
8. B–Q3	B–KT2
9. KT–K5 (Fig C)	. . . . . .

Now White's threat of **10. Q–R5 ch** is very strong. If **10. . . . . . ., P–KT3** then **11. KT x**

P, P x KT; **12. Q x P ch** and wins the Bishop.

9.	O–O
10. Q–R5	. . . . . .

Black is in real trouble now. If **10. . . . . . .,** **QB x KT; 11. B x B, P–KR3; 12. B x R.**

10.	Q–K2 (Fig D)
11. Q x P ch	K x Q

Black is forced to take the Queen.

12. KT x B dble ch	. . . . . .

Here is the double check. Black can not go back to R1 because then **13. KT–KT6** is checkmate. It is also a nice three way fork.

12.	K–R3
13. KT(K5)–KT4 ch	K–KT4
14. P–KR4 ch	K–B5
15. P–KKT3 ch	K–B6
16. B–K2 ch	K–KT7
17. R–R2 ch	K–KT8
18. K–Q2 mate.	

The discovered check move **18** wins the game. When White played **11. Q x P ch** every move for Black was forced until the checkmate.

End Game-1

This is the part of the game when most of the pieces have been taken off the board. Most of the danger to the King has gone and he can come out of his safe corner and join in the battle. To win the game the King must be helped by at least one Queen, or one Rook, or two Bishops, or one Bishop and one Knight, or three Knights or one Pawn.

Let's look at some very simple end games.

King with Queen against King
Look at **Fig A** and **Fig B**. Even a piece as powerful as the Queen needs help from the King. Be very careful not to get a position as shown on **Fig C** if it is Black's turn to move. That would be stalemate.

Let's see how to get the enemy King into a position like **Fig A** or **B**. Look at **Fig D**. All the squares on the rank and file extending from the Queen are coloured red. The Black King will never be able to move to any of the squares.

White to move plays **1. Q–B3 (Fig E)**. Now the red lines extending from the Queen form a barrier to the Black King. It can never get out of the square bounded by red squares. Black plays **1. ......, K–Q3.**

Now White plays **2. Q–K4 (Fig F)**. Look how the area bounded by the red squares has grown smaller.

Black plays **2. ......, K–B2.**

White plays **3. Q–Q5 (Fig G)**. Now the Black King is in a prison of nine squares. Even three of those squares are forbidden to him as they are controlled by the White Queen.

It does not matter where the Black King goes in his little prison. White just brings up his own King until he supports the Queen, and then gives checkmate. Let's start at **Fig D** again and look at all the moves.

WHITE	BLACK
1. Q–B3	K–Q3
2. Q–K4	K–B2
3. Q–Q5	K–KT3
4. K–KT2	K–R2
5. K–KT3	K–KT3
6. K–KT4	K–R3
7. Q–B6 ch	K–R2 (forced)
8. K–R5	K–KT1 (forced)
9. Q–Q7	......

White must not play **9. K–KT6** because it is stalemate.

9.	K–R1 (forced)
10. K–KT6	K–KT1 (forced)

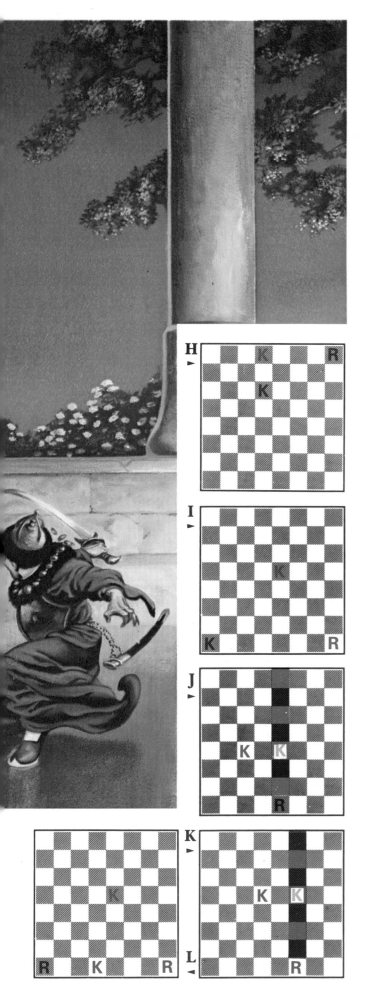

And now White mates with **11. Q–Q8** or **11. Q–K8** or **11. Q–KT7**.

This is not the shortest way to checkmate but it shows you the idea. You can use that idea again and again in the end game.

King and Rook against King

Look at **Fig H**. This is the checkmate position you are looking for in this sort of end game.

As the Rook is not as powerful as the Queen, you must bring up your King first. Then cut off the enemy King with the Rook using the rank or file. Look at **Fig I**. Here's one way.

WHITE	BLACK
1. K–KT2	K–Q4
2. K–B3	K–K4
3. K–B4	K–K5
4. R–K1 ch (Fig J)	. . . . . .

In **Fig J** the Black King is forced to move to the right into the King's Bishop file.

4.	K–B4
5. K–Q4	K–B3
6. K–Q5	K–B4
7. R–B1 ch (Fig K)	. . . . . .

Fig K is just like **Fig J** only it has all been moved one file to the right. Now the Black King has to move into the King's Knight file.

7.	K–KT3
8. K–K5	K–KT4
9. R–KT1 ch	. . . . . .

This time we won't bother with a diagram. If we had it would look just like **Fig K** only all the pieces would be moved one file to the right. This time the Black King has to move to the Rook file.

9.	K–R4
10. K–B4	K–R3
11. K–B5	K–R2
12. K–B6	K–R1
13. K–B7	. . . . . .

This time the Black King can't run away any longer as he is in the corner.

13.	K–R2
14. R–R1 mate.	

The mate is just like **Fig H.**

King with Two Rooks against the King

This time checkmate is very easy. Look at **Fig L**.

WHITE	BLACK
1. R–QR4	K–B4
2. R–KR5 ch	K–KT3
3. R–KT5	K–B3
4. R–QR6 ch	K–K2
5. R–KT7 ch	K–Q1
6. R–R8 mate.	

End Game - 2

King with two Bishops against King

Because the Bishops move on the diagonals, you must force the enemy King into a corner. First you must bring up your King to help.

Let's start with **Fig A** and look at the moves. This time it is the White King that is to be mated so do not forget that Black plays downwards in the diagram.

WHITE	BLACK
1.	K–KT2
2. K–Q4	K–B3
3. K–K4	K–B4
4. K–K3	K–B5
5. K–K4	B–B6
6. K–K3	B–Q5 ch
7. K–K4	B–K7 (Fig B)

This is a very important position. The White King is forced to move to the right into the King's Bishop file. The two Bishops and the King are forcing the White King to the edge of the board. The Blue arrows coming from the Bishops show how few squares the White King has left to choose. It is just like the King and Rook against King ending.

| 8. K–B4 | K–Q4 |
| 9. K–B5 | B–K4 (Fig C) |

Fig C is very like **Fig B** but this time the White King is forced to move to the right into the King's Knight file. Now we will repeat this pattern of moves until the White King is at the edge of the board.

| 10. K–KT5 | K–K3 |
| 11. K–KT6 | B–B3 |

Again the pattern we know so well now. We will not bother with a diagram this time. The White King is forced into the Rook file at last.

| 12. K–R6 | K–B2 |
| 13. K–R7 | B–K2 |

This time Black cannot play the move you expect, **B–KT2**. That would be stalemate.

| 14. K–R6 | B–B6 |

Black's fourteenth move is very important. It is called a waiting move. The position is still really the same but now White has to move again. He doesn't really want to but of course the rules say that he must.

| 15. K–R7 | B–KT4 |
| 16. K–R8 (forced) | B–K7 |

Another waiting move. Black has set up the position for mating and now White is forced into the trap.

| 17. K–R7 | B–Q6 ch |
| 18. K–R8 | B–B3 mate. |

King with Bishop and Knight against King

This ending is very difficult. The King has to be driven to the corner which has the same colour square as the Bishop. **Fig D** shows the mating position. It may take 34 moves to get mate so you can see that the 50 move rule is necessary.

King with Three Knights against King

You have already seen that you can have three Knights from the section on pawn promotion. You could also have three Queens if you were lucky! **Fig E** shows the mating position. It can take up to twenty moves to get such a mate. These last two mating positions in the end game are hardly ever seen, so let's turn to one which is fairly common.

King and Pawn against King

Obviously this type of ending can only be won if the pawn can be promoted. If the Black King is too far away to stop the pawn then White wins. Look at **Fig F**. This is called the 'Queening Square'. This is a quick way to work out whether you can catch the pawn or not. If the Black King is inside the 'Queening Square', it can always stop the pawn. In the position in **Fig F**, if it was Black to move; he would move inside the square and catch the pawn. If it was White's move then the pawn would be promoted before the Black King could catch it. Try it out a few times on your own board.

'The Opposition'

Most King and pawn endings are a battle between the two Kings. One tries to force his pawn through to the eighth rank and promotion. The other tries to stop the pawn (**Fig G**).

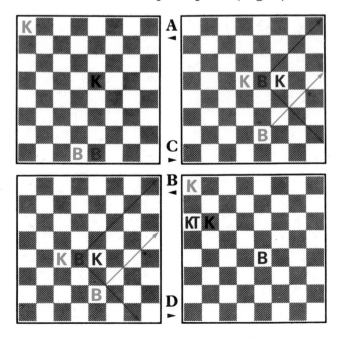

The rules of chess keep the Kings at least one square apart. This means that they can block each other. In **Fig G** the White King cannot move up the board if it is White to move. The Black King cannot move down the board.

Let's suppose it is Black's move. If he tries to stop White's King advancing the best he can do is play **1. . . . . . . , K–KT4** or **1. . . . . . . , K–K4**. To the first White would play **2. K–K4**, and to the second **2. K–KT4**. So White who had what we call 'the opposition' is now up to the fourth rank. Black could not stop the advance. 'The opposition' is really the power to make the other King step aside. It belongs to the side which does not have the move.

In **Fig G** it is called Vertical Opposition. It can also be Horizontal Opposition where the two Kings fight over a file instead of a rank. Or it can be Diagonal opposition.

Let's see this 'opposition' in action in a King and pawn against King ending. **Fig H** has Black to play.

1.	K–K3
2. K–KT5	K–K4
3. P–B4 ch	K–K3
4. K–KT6	K–K2
5. P–B5	K–B1
6. K–B6	. . . . . .

White regains the opposition.

6.	K–KT1
7. K–K7	

Now the White King controls the queening square B8. The pawn can be brought through.

Your chance of winning this sort of ending is always better if you can keep your King in front of your pawn. At least one square in front of your pawn and the opposition guarantees a win.

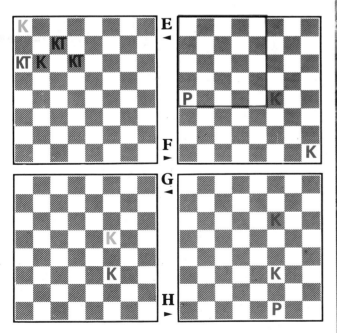

Openings-1

The first ten or so moves in a game are called the opening. This is the part of the game where each player tries to place his pieces in the best position for the coming battle.

Bringing your pieces out from the back rank is called 'developing'. There are lots of different openings and they all have their own names. You have seen some of them already like 'The Dutch Defence', 'The Scotch Game' and 'Philidor's Defence'. These names tell you where the opening became popular or who made it famous. Sometimes the name tells us something about the opening like 'The King's Gambit'.

Chess has been played and recorded for a very long time so most ideas in the openings are well known. It is important that you should not try to 're-invent the wheel' when you play an opening. You should not spend ages trying to find the best move when the whole world already knows what it is. On the other hand there is no point in memorizing long lists of moves if you do not understand why they are being played. The best thing you can do is to try to understand what the opening is about; what the ideas behind the moves mean. If you understand the ideas, you will soon find the moves. There are two main ideas that apply to nearly all openings. One is rapid development and the other, centre control. Here are some general tips that will help you understand these two ideas.

1. Develop all your pieces as fast as you can. Develop towards the centre and not the edge of the board.
2. Try to move either your King's pawn or Queen's pawn to the fourth rank and keep it there. Don't make any more pawn moves unless you have to.
3. Don't move any pieces twice before you have developed all your pieces.
4. Don't exchange a piece which is developed for one that isn't.
5. Don't block your own pieces. Especially don't block in a centre pawn. Let's look at an opening and the ideas behind it.

'THE KING'S GAMBIT'

WHITE	BLACK
A. Planinc	V. Korchnoi
1. P–K4	P–K4
2. P–KB4	P x P

This opening has a clear plan. White is

aiming at Black's weakest square KB2. Giving up the pawn clears the King's Bishop file. First White will play **KT–KB3** to stop Black's **Q–R5**. Second he will develop his King's Bishop. Third he will castle King's side and then the Rook will be standing on KB1. Look at **Fig A**. White's Bishop and Knight (which is moved to K5 or KT5) aim at Black's KB2. Only the Rook is blocked in its attack by the Black pawn at White's KB4. White's plan is clear, he must get the Black pawn out of the way.

Let's look at **Fig A** again. White has made six moves and Black only two. The diagram was shown in this way to make White's plan easier to understand. What would Black do? The opposite of White's plan is the answer. He must keep his pawn on the King's Bishop file to block the Rook.

3. KT–KB3	P–KKT4
4. P–KR4	. . . . . .

Black supports his forward pawn. White attacks the defending Knight pawn.

4.	P–KT5
5. KT–K5	P–Q3
6. KT x KTP	KT–KB3
7. KT–B2	R–KT1

White could have played **7. KT x KT ch**, which Korchnoi, the great Russian player, gives as the best move in his book on the opening.

| 8. P–Q4 | B–R3 (Fig B) |

Look at **Fig B**. White's plan of attack at Black's KB2 has failed. Black supports his forward pawn with his Bishop. Black's Rook ties White's Bishop to the defence of his Knight's pawn. However White has pawns at

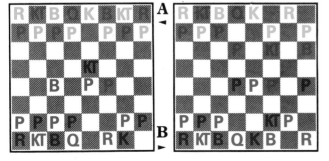

Q4 and K4—an advantage.

9. KT–B3	Q–K7
10. KT–Q3	B–KT5
11. B–K2	B x B
12. Q x B	KT–B3

Development of the pieces for both sides is almost complete. Black's exchange of the White-squared Bishops means that White will have problems defending his King's Knight pawn. White's Queen pawn is under attack but he can now win the pawn at KB4.

13. B x P	KT x QP
14. Q–B2	KT x KP
15. KT x KT	Q x KT ch
16. K–Q1	. . . . . .

White threatens **17. R–K1** pinning the Queen

| 16. . . . . . . | O–O–O |
| 17. B x B | R x P |

Black's move invades the seventh rank. Look how his Rook attacks all along the seventh rank.

| 18. Q–B1 | KT x P |
| 19. R–B1 | Q–KT5 ch |

White resigns.

Openings-2

The Ruy Lopez

This opening was named after the Spanish priest who wrote about it in one of the first chess books in 1561.

The game we are going to look at (to see how the first moves are made) was played in 1976. Nigel Short, who had the White pieces, was just twelve years old when the game was played. In 1977. Nigel, still twelve, was the youngest player ever to compete in the British Championship. In 1979 he tied for first place.

WHITE	BLACK
N. Short	**G. Knapton**

RUY LOPEZ

1.	P–K4	P–K4
2.	KT–KB3	KT–QB3
3.	B–KT5 (**Fig A**)	. . . . . .

These are the moves that begin the Ruy Lopez. The object, of course, is to gain control of the centre board. If White could get rid of Black's pawn and play **P–Q4**, the two pawns in the centre would be a great advantage. To do so he plays **3. B–KT5** attacking the Black Knight. This is the only defender of the Black King's pawn, so by attacking the defender he is really attacking the pawn.

What would happen if White played **4. B x KT**? Then Black would reply **4. . . . . . . QP x B**; and now White wins the Black KP with **5. KT x P** (**Fig B**). No! He doesn't! You see Black would reply **5. . . . . . . , Q–Q5**! This move attacks the White Knight and King's pawn at the same time. As White can't save them both with one move he has to give up the pawn (it's worth less than the Knight).

So **3. B–KT5** is not a real threat. It will become a threat when White defends his King's pawn.

3.	. . . . . .	P–QR3 (**Fig C**)

This move is seen in lots of games. It's called 'putting the question to the Bishop'. What Black is saying by attacking the Bishop with **3. . . . . . . , P–QR3** is: 'Are you going to exchange the Bishop for the Knight or not? If you retreat to QR4, then I will play **P–QKT4** so this is your last chance to play **B x KT**.'

4.	B–R4	KT–B3

Black decides to attack the undefended King's pawn first.

5.	P–Q4	P–QKT4
6.	B–KT3	B–K2

Here Black makes a mistake. White's opening of the game needs a more active answer.

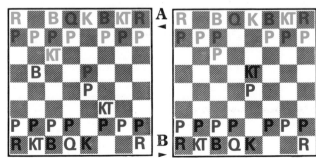

36

6. . . . . . . , P x P is best.

7. P x P (Fig D) . . . . .

Black cannot play **7. . . . . . . , KKT x P.** as **8. Q–Q5** wins a piece for White (It threatens checkmate on Black's KB2 square.)

7. . . . . . .   **KKT–KT5**

8. P–KR3   . . . . . .

Black still cannot take a pawn. If **8. . . . . . . , KT (KT5) x P,** then **9. KT x KT, KT x KT**; **10. Q–Q5 (Fig E).**

A real fork! White threatens to take the Rook and the Knight. If the Knight moves, **Q x BP** is checkmate.

8. . . . . . .   **KT–R3**

So Black has to play his Knight to the edge of the board.

9. KT–B3	**O–O**
10. O–O	**P–Q3**
11. P x P	**Q x P**
12. Q–K2	**Q–KT3**

A nasty threat! Black will play **13. . . . . . . , B x P.** White would'nt be able to play **14. P x B** as the pawn is pinned by the Black Queen on Black KKT3.

13. KT–Q5   . . . . . .

The threat is stifled. If Black plays **13. . . . . . . , B x P,** White would reply **14. KT–B4** and the Black Bishop is lost.

13. . . . . . .   **R–Q1 ?**

The question mark (?) means that this is a bad move. White shows why with his next move.

14. KT–K5 (Fig F)   . . . . . .

Now the Black Queen is attacked. She has only two safe moves left. Can you see what they are ?

One is **Q–K3** and the other is the move Black played. Neither prevents White winning.

Why did'nt Black play **14. . . . . . . , KT x KT** ? Well as you can see in **Fig F**, White would play **15. KT x B ch** and fork the King and Queen.

14. . . . . . .   **Q–Q3**

15. KT x KT   **Resigns**

Black resigns. If he played **15. . . . . . . , Q x KT (B3)**; then **16. KT x B ch** and once again the fork of the King and Queen wins.

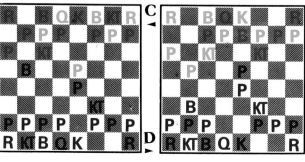

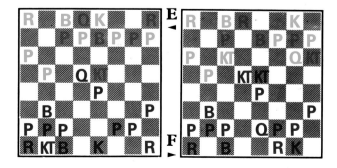

Openings-3

The Queen's Gambit

To introduce this opening we are going to look at the first game of the 1978 World Championship match. Although it is a very old opening, it was used six times in this match.

The order of moves in this game has been changed to make the opening easier to understand. This is called 'transposing'. Players often transpose the moves in an opening to confuse their opponents. This is a good reason not to learn the opening moves by heart. Try to learn the ideas behind the opening moves. Once you know the idea, then the moves come easily.

WHITE	BLACK
V. Korchnoi	A. Karpov

QUEEN'S GAMBIT

1. P–Q4	P–Q4
2. P–QB4	. . . . . .

This is a bit like looking at the King's Gambit in a mirror. Still there are some very important differences. Firstly the Queen's pawn is protected by the Queen. Secondly, the White King is not so open to attack. The Queen, Queen's Knight and Bishop can come to its aid on the Queen's side. Thirdly, it will take White longer to castle. On the King's side there are only two pieces to move out of the way before castling. On the Queen's side, there are three.

In the King's Gambit White could not play **3. P x P** because Black had the terrible reply **3. . . . . . . , Q–R5 ch**. This time White does threaten **3. P x P** because if Black replies **3. . . . . . . , Q x P**; then **4. KT–QB3**, the Queen moves; **5. P–K4**. White would have pawns at K4 and Q4; a big advantage.

2.	P–K3

Black decides to keep a pawn at Q4 whatever happens.

3. KT–QB3	KT–KB3

Both players develop Knights. White's Knight attacks the Queen's pawn; Black's Knight defends his Queen's pawn and prevents White's future **P–K4**.

4. B–KT5	B–K2

White pins the Black Knight and also strengthens his attack on the Black Queen's pawn. Black unpins right away (**Fig A**).

Black could play **4. . . . . . . , QKT–Q2**. It would be equally good. It also sets a trap. After **4. . . . . . . , QKT–Q2** it looks as if White can win a pawn. **5. P x P, P x P; 6. KT x P?, KT x KT; 7. B x Q, B–KT5 ch**; now White

has to give up his Queen. **8. Q–Q2, B x Q ch; 9. K x B, K x B**. Black wins a Knight for a pawn.

5. P–K3	O–O

White opens the way for his King's Bishop. Black castles bringing his Rook into play and finding safety for his King.

6. KT–B3	P–KR3
7. B–R4	P–QKT3

White has developed his King's Knight and Black puts the question to the White Queen's Bishop. After White's Bishop retreats to KR4, the Queen's Knight pawn move of Black leads to a type of Queen's Gambit Declined called 'Tartkover's Defence'.

From this point on we play the moves in the same order as the two grandmasters.

8. R–B1	B–KT2
9. B–Q3	P x P
10. B x P	QKT–Q2
11. O–O	P–B4. (Fig B)

In this position you can see that both players

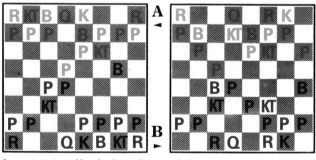

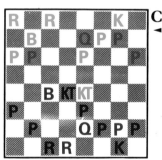

have got all their pieces into the game (they have developed). All the pieces stand on good squares. The position is evenly balanced.

12.	P x P	KT x P
13.	Q–K2	P–R3
14.	KR–Q1	Q–K1
15.	P–QR3	KKT–K5
16.	KT x KT	KT x KT
17.	B x B	Q x B
18.	KT–Q4	KR–B1 (Fig C)

At this point the World Champion, Karpov offered a draw which Korchnoi accepted.

Both grandmasters had reached this sort of position many times before and decided that further play would gain them nothing. This is an example of an agreed draw.

You should not copy the example of great players like Karpov and Korchnoi while you are learning to play chess. Always try to win. If you lose at least you will learn something; and perhaps you will win.

Karpov eventually won the 1978 match and retained his World Championship, although there were 21 drawn games.

Openings-4

The Sicilian Defence

The game we are going to look at in order to learn about this opening was played in 1948. At the time the game was played, Viktor Korchnoi (White) was 17 years old. His opponent Boris Spassky was 11 years old. Both players later went on to challenge for the World Championship. Korchnoi failed narrowly in 1978, losing to Karpov. Spassky won the World Championship in 1969. He lost the title to Bobby Fischer in 1972.

WHITE	BLACK
V. Korchnoi	B. Spassky

SICILIAN DEFENCE

1. P–K4   P–QB4

Black does not copy White's first move. His pawn is waiting for White to try to play **2. P–Q4.**

What would happen if he did? **2. P–Q4, P x P; 3. Q x P, KT–QB3**! Look at **Fig A.** Black's third move **KT–QB3** attacks the White Queen. So White has to lose time by moving the Queen to safety. **2. P–Q4** would not be a good move now. Perhaps White can play it later.

Let's go back to the game. Did you see that Black can move his Queen now? He won't be able to move a Bishop and he will not be able to play **2. . . . . . , P–Q4** either.

What would happen if he did? **2. P–KKT3** (any move will do), **P–Q4; 3. P x P, Q x P; 4. KT–QB3, ...** This time the Black Queen has to move again.

Back to the game.

2. KT–KB3   P–Q3

White plays to prepare **3. P–Q4.** Black's move stops the King's pawn advancing. It allows Black's Queen's Knight to move to Q2 or QB3. It also allows the Queen's Bishop to move.

3. P–Q4   P x P
4. KT x P   KT–KB3

So White gets his pawn back. Black attacks the King's pawn and at the same time brings out the King's Knight. Did you notice that Black's first three moves were all with pawns? Because of Black's second move **2. . . . . . , P–Q3,** the White King's pawn cannot advance **5. P–K5** and so:

5. KT–QB3   . . . . . .

White brings out his Queen's Knight. At the same time he defends his pawn.

5. . . . . . .   P–KKT3 (Fig B)

This move by Black is very popular. It starts a type of Sicilian Defence that is called 'The Dragon Variation'.

Let's see how both sides are getting on in the opening. White has two Knights out. Both his Bishops can move. He has a pawn at K4. His Queen's file is half-open. That means that he has no pawn on the Queen's file so he can attack down that file with a Rook later.

Black will play **B–KT2** soon. His Queen's Bishop file is half open. He will attack with a Rook down this file later. His King's Knight is out. His Queen's pawn is at Q3. His Queen's Bishop can move. This position is very well known. Both sides have equal chances.

Back to the game.

6. P–KB4   B–KT5

White starts a pawn attack on the King's side. Black attacks the White Queen.

7. B–KT5 ch   QKT–Q2

Black puts his Knight in the way to stop the check.

8. B x KT ch   Q x B
9. Q–Q3   . . . . . .

This is a good move. He gets his Queen away

from the Black Bishop and at the same time gets ready to play **10. P–B5**.

  9. . . . . . .   **P–K4**

This move attacks the White Knight at Q4. It stops White playing **P–B5**.

10. KT–B3   **B x KT**

11. Q x B   **Q–KT5**??

Black's move gets two question marks. A real blunder. It lost the game. Can you see why?

12. KT–Q5   **Resigns** (Fig C)

Of course! If Black plays **12. . . . . . .**, **Q x Q** then **13. KT x KT** check followed by **Q x Q** wins a piece.

If Black plays **12. . . . . . .**, **KT x KT** to stop the fork at KB7 (did you notice that threat?) then **13. Q x Q** and he loses a Queen for a Knight.

The eleven-year-old Spassky later became World Champion so it shows you that anybody can make a mistake.

The trick is to learn from the mistakes you make.

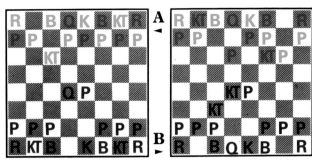

Great Players and Their Games

Alexander Alekhine

One of the best players ever. He won the World Championship in 1927 from Capablanca who was considered unbeatable at that time. He later lost the title to Max Euwe in 1935 but regained it in 1937. He was still World Champion at his death in 1946.

His opponent in this game, the author of 'My System', was a great player and one of the most important writers in chess literature.

WHITE	BLACK
Alekhine	Nimzowitsch
FRENCH DEFENCE	
1. P–K4	P–K3
2. P–Q4	P–Q4
3. KT–QB3	B–KT5
4. KKT–K2	P x P
5. P–QR3	B x KT ch
6. KT x B	P–KB4
7. P–B3	P x P
8. Q x P	Q x P
9. Q–KT3	KT–KB3
10. Q x KTP	Q–K4 ch
11. B–K2	R–KT1
12. Q–R6	R–KT3
13. Q–R4	B–Q2
14. B–KKT5	B–B3
15. O–O–O	B x P
16. KR–K1	B–K5
17. B–R5	KT x B
18. R–Q8 ch	K–B2
19. Q x KT	Resigns.

Fig A.

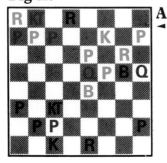

▲ *Boris Spassky*

Mikhail Tal.

One of the most exciting players in the world. His game is full of sacrifices. He won the World Championship in 1960 when he was 23 years old. The youngest winner of the title. Sadly, ill health affected his play after his title win. He lost the title in 1961 in a re-match with Botvinnik. Recently he has shown a welcome return to form.

WHITE	BLACK
Tal	Milev
QUEEN'S GAMBIT DECLINED	
(Transposed)	
1. P–QB4	P–QB4
2. KT–QB3	KT–QB3
3. KT–B3	KT–B3
4. P–K3	P–K3
5. P–Q4	P–Q4
6. BP x P	KKT x P
7. B–B4	KT–KT3
8. B–KT5	P–QR3
9. B x KT ch	P x B
10. O–O	B–KT2
11. KT–K4	KT–Q2
12. Q–B2	Q–KT3
13. KT–K5	P x P
14. KT x KT	K x KT
15. P x P	K–K1
16. B–K3	Q–B2
17. P–Q5	KP x P
18. KR–K1	K–Q1
19. Q–KT3	P–QB4
20. KT x P	Resigns

Fig. B.

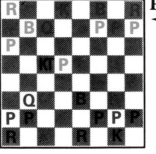

▲ *Bobby Fisher*

Boris Spassky

The World Champion from 1969 until 1972 when he lost the title to Bobby Fischer in a match which set the chess world alight. This game which Spassky won was the eleventh of that match. A brilliant win by one of the world's strongest grandmasters. This game was also Fischer's last defeat.

WHITE	BLACK
Spassky	Fischer
SICILIAN DEFENCE	
1. P–K4	P–QB4
2. KT–KB3	P–Q3
3. P–Q4	P x P
4. KT x P	KT–KB3
5. KT–QB3	P–QR3
6. B–KKT5	P–K3

7. P–B4	Q–KT3
8. Q–Q2	Q x P
9. KT–KT3	Q–R6
10. B x KT	P x B
11. B–K2	P–KR4
12. O–O	KT–B3
13. K–R1	B–Q2
14. KT–KT1	Q–KT5
15. Q–K3	P–Q4
16. P x P	KT–K2
17. P–B4	KT–B4
18. Q–Q3	P–R5
19. B–KT4	KT–Q3
20. KT(1)–Q2	P–B4
21. P–QR3	Q–KT3
22. P–B5	Q–KT4
23. Q–QB3	P x B
24. P–R4	P–R6
25. P x Q	P x P ch
26. K x P	R–R6
27. Q–B6	KT–B4
28. P–B6	B–B1
29. QP x P	BP x P
30. KR–K1	B–K2
31. R x P	Resigns.

Fig C.

▲ *Anatoly Karpov*

Bobby Fischer

He won the World Championship in 1972 in the famous match with Spassky. F.I.D.E., the governing body of World Chess, stripped him of the title in 1975 after a dispute. He is still regarded as the best player in the world by many people although he hasn't played since his World Championship win. He won the U.S. championship when he was 14 years old. He was a grandmaster at 15 years of age. The youngest ever holder of the title.

WHITE	BLACK
R. Byrne	Fischer
GRUENFELD DEFENCE	
1. P–Q4	KT–KB3
2. P–QB4	P–KKT3
3. P–KKT3	P–B3
4. B–KT2	P–Q4
5. P x P	P x P

6. KT–QB3	B–KT2
7. P–K3	O–O
8. KKT–K2	KT–B3
9. O–O	P–KT3
10. P–KT3	B–QR3
11. B–QR3	R–K1
12. Q–Q2	P–K4
13. P x P	KT x P
14. KR–Q1	KT–Q6
15. Q–B2	KT x P
16. K x KT	KT–KT5 ch
17. K–KT1	KT x KP
18. Q–Q2	KT x B
19. K x KT	P–Q5
20. KT x P	B–KT2 ch
21. K–B1	Q–Q2

White resigned.
Fig D.

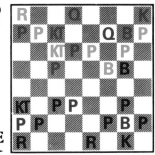

Anatoly Karpov

The present World Champion. He won the World Championship Candidates Tournament in 1974 beating Korchnoi in the final and was awarded the World Championship in 1975. He defended his title successfully against Korchnoi in 1978. The game below is from the World Junior Championship which he won in 1969. Past winners of the title include Spassky and Britain's Tony Miles.

WHITE	BLACK
Karpov	Payrhuber
SICILIAN DEFENCE	
1. P–K4	P–QB4
2. KT–KB3	P–Q3
3. P–KKT3	KT–KB3
4. P–Q3	KT–B3
5. B–KT2	P–KKT3
6. O–O	B–KT2
7. R–K1	O–O
8. P–B3	KT–K1
9. KT–R3	P–B4
10. KT–KKT5	KT–B2
11. Q–KT3 ch	K–R1
12. P x P	QB x P
13. KT–B7 ch	R x KT
14. Q x R	P–K3
15. B–KT5	Resigns.

Fig E.

Hints for Young Players

If you have read and played your way through as far as this last section, you are already on the way to playing chess well and enjoying and understanding other people's games. One thing this book cannot do is to give you chess practice. You must play often and regularly. To do this you should join your school chess club. Always try to play against opponents who are stronger players than yourself. You will learn more from losing to a stronger player than you will ever learn from winning against weaker ones. Don't be afraid to lose. Losing is learning.

If chess doesn't interfere with your school work join the local chess club as well as the school club. If your school doesn't have a chess club ask if one can be started. Soon you will be playing in matches against other teams. This is real chess. You will be playing against the clock and you will have to record the moves.

Your chess club will probably have tournaments so you will be able to compete against other players in serious games.

Now that you can read and write chess notation, you will be able to read newspaper articles. You will be surprised how many newspapers and magazines have a chess section or column. Look through some in your local library.

You will want to watch any chess programmes on Television. Keep a look out for any that might appear. Chess on T.V. is particularly interesting to watch.

Young people to-day who want to play chess have one big advantage over those in the past years. The world of electronics has produced chess playing machines. Although these are relatively expensive the price is coming down all the time. If you are lucky enough to have one, you will be able to use it for chess practice. Don't forget that chess is really a game to be played between two **people**. Playing against a machine is not quite the same.

Most chess players buy chess magazines regularly. They tell you what is happening in your local area and also throughout the world.

You will find games from the best players in the world and results of important tournaments. Articles explaining opening theory are very useful and many magazines often have such articles. Ask your newsagent about them.

When you feel that you would like to improve your game, look for chess books which will help you. Leonard Barden's book **'Play Better Chess'** is a good example. There are lots of others as there have been more books written about chess than all the other board games put together. Pay special attention to any books on the end game. That is the part of the game which most people play poorly when they begin chess.

When you start to play seriously (perhaps at school or at your local chess club), always write down the game. Afterwards play through the game and see if you can make any improvements in your play or your opponent's. Discuss the game with your opponent when it is over. See if he thinks the same about the moves. Perhaps he will have a different idea. Chess is a game of ideas.

You will find details of chess tournaments in the chess magazines. Try to visit a tournament when there's one near you. You'll be fascinated to watch hundreds of people, all playing chess at the same time. Some of the important games will have big chess display boards showing the position the game has reached so you can see the game as it is played. You will also be able to see well known players in action.

Perhaps you will decide to play in one of the tournaments yourself. They have competitions at all levels, so there's bound to be one that will suit you. Always start off your tournament career by playing in the easiest section.

One final point. Never try to annoy your opponent during a game. When it is his turn to move, you must be quiet. There are special rules to cover behaviour in serious games. You will learn then with experience but basically what they mean is that you must treat your opponent as you would like to be treated by him.

Good luck in all your chess games!

Tony Hansford